Small Changes, Great Impact

OrangeBooks Publication

Smriti Nagar, Bhilai, Chhattisgarh - 490020

Website: **www.orangebooks.in**

© Copyright, 2023, Author

All rights reserved. No part of this book may be reproduced, stored in a retrieval system, or transmitted, in any form by any means, electronic, mechanical, magnetic, optical, chemical, manual, photocopying, recording or otherwise, without the prior written consent of its writer.

First Edition, 2023

SMALL CHANGES, GREAT IMPACT

A GUIDE TO CHANGE THE WORLD

Rajat Sharma

OrangeBooks Publication
www.orangebooks.in

Preface

Dear Reader,

With great excitement I have brought this book to you, It explores what we can do in life to change our life and the world around us.

This book is not an autobiography, but rather a tool for change. I have included personal incidents only to inspire and motivate you, as I consider you part of my family. The focus is on the lessons the book imparts, so please read with that in mind

All of us complain that there are problems in our life and in the world, but what do we do about it?

This book will give a check-sheet of how I changed my life and How you can do it too. Everyone talks about problems and solution but I'm not going to do the same thing. I want to present you the solution in ways which you can implement. I don't want to tell big sentences or essays. I want to simplify things and tell things which we can actually do.

So if you are ready on the journey to seeing life as a game and scoring your points then continue reading the book.

I hope this book inspires you to take action and be the change you want to see

__Sincerely,__

Rajat Sharma

Content

1. Introduction 1
2. Personal Pivots 5
   - Meditation 9
   - Bhagavad gita 24
   - Exercise 30
   - A story of a beautiful girl 41
3. Improve community 44
   - Gratitude 48
   - Spread smiles and happiness 55
4. Social spark-plugs 58
   - Orphanage and old age homes 58
   - Hospitals 61
5. National navigators 65
   - Cleanliness 65
   - Helping the poor 68
6. Global game changers 74
   - Be a Vegan 74
7. Conclusion 81
8. Check-sheets 85

Introduction

Lot of people ask me what are the problems that I can solve in today's world, How can I help the society, What can I do for this world. You will get answers to all these questions as you read the book.

Do you know what is the difference between Humans and animals??

We are Intelligent and have consciousness. Have you ever thought about it that why we have such a good body and consciousness? Is it only for basic needs?? Are you born only to work daily like Animals do and get your meals and Have a shelter and buy clothes??

We may be intelligent but still almost everyone works for food or for family. People who are rich successful also work for same thing. They may have a good quality of life. They might spend more for same things. They may wear better clothes, Better house, Better Food but ultimately they do same things. Aren't animals Living for the same things???

So What should we do?? How can we make use of this body in better way??

Just one word answer will - Finding purpose of Life

Why do we remember Dr.B.R.Ambedkar, Abdul Kalam, Mahatma Gandhi, Nelson Mandela etc. We remember these people because they didn't just live for themself like everyone does. And that my friend is the purpose of life. We must bring a change. We must realize what is the difference between good and bad. Most people don't realize this. Most people do same thing that everyone is doing.

Do you know when Blacks were mistreated why no one fought?? Do you know why no one fought for the Dalits in India for a long time??

Because people don't even realize they are doing something wrong. Imagine seeing those things from childhood and not being told its wrong, won't you think that its normal to mistreat those lower-class people. That's the reason why we must read this book. We must train ourself to think beyond what is considered normal. Only then we will be able to do something that is different and something that is ultimately right.

But most people think you need power, you need money, you need extra time to change our life and the world, But that's not true. Small changes in our daily life can help change world and also our own life.

As you dive deeper into this book you will completely start to become a different person, A person who thinks different and who sees the world differently and all these will happen from the first day, from the day you implement it.

Every day, people across the world face a wide range of challenges and problems, from poverty and homelessness to climate change and political conflict. Despite these issues, it often feels like we are not doing enough to make a meaningful difference. We are surrounded by suffering and hardship, yet we seem to be paralyzed by inaction, watching from the sidelines as the world falls apart around us.

Think about it, every time we turn on the news, we are bombarded with stories of natural disasters, war, and suffering. We see images of families torn apart by conflict, of communities ravaged by famine, of children dying from preventable diseases. It's heart-wrenching and overwhelming, and it's easy to feel like there's nothing we can do to make a difference.

But, what if I told you that we have the power to change all of this? What if I told you that each and every one of us can make a difference, simply by making small changes in our own lives?

Take, for example, the story of a young girl. She lived in a small village in India, and she had always dreamed of going to school. But, there was no school in her village, and her parents could not afford to send her to the nearest one. Her future looked bleak, until one day, a kind stranger came to her village and built a school. That school changed her life forever. She was able to get an education, and she went on to become a teacher, inspiring countless other children just like her.

Yes, I know it is not possible for us to construct a school and help people but what if I told you about things you can do. There are so many things which we can do to bring change in your life and also others life.

By building a school, one person was able to change the lives of countless children. And, that's just the beginning. By taking small steps in our own lives, we can work together to create a better world for everyone.

So, I encourage you to take a look at your own life and ask yourself, "What small changes can I make to create a better world?" Whether it's volunteering at a local shelter, reducing your carbon footprint, or simply spreading kindness and positivity, every small action we take can bring us one step closer to a better world. Let's not turn a blind eye to the problems of our world anymore. It's time for us to take action and make a meaningful difference.

Personal Pivots

Small shifts that transform your life

As a school student, I was blissfully unaware of the small things in life. My world was one which revolved around creativity. I was a natural learner, devouring knowledge like a sponge and seeing the world through a unique lens. I was passionate about people and had a lot of hobbies, including painting and crafting. My young hands were never still, constantly creating drawings and imaginative projects without the distraction of the internet. I was truly living the meaning of creativity.

But now, I see how the internet has taken away the spark of originality and creativity in others. People have grown dependent on instant gratification, losing the joy of the creative process. Lucky for me, I had the privilege of growing up without this digital crutch. This allowed me to savor the sweetness of life and bask in my imagination.

As I transitioned into pre-university college, everything changed. The once-innocent world I inhabited became a place of temptation and vice. I was surrounded by individuals who saw nothing wrong with smoking and drinking. Despite my attempts to educate and discourage these habits, many argue that it is simply a personal choice. But I ask you this: what happened to the childlike wonder and pure heart that we all once possessed? Where has the spark of creativity gone? Why have we allowed ourselves to be consumed by destructive behaviors? It is time to rediscover the joys of youth and reclaim the innocence that once defined us.

As I engage with smokers and drinkers, I am constantly curious about their motivations. I ask the question, "Why do you smoke? Why do you drink?" The answers are as varied as the individuals themselves, with some saying that life is short and they want to experience everything at least once.

To them, I say just one thing: *why not taste poison just once?*

The destructive nature of these habits is not a source of enjoyment, but rather a slow, painful demise. So, I implore you to reconsider and rediscover the thrill of living life to its fullest, free from the shackles of addiction.

Stress is often cited as a reason for indulging in destructive habits like smoking and drinking. But let's reflect on our childhoods, where we faced pressures from various sources, yet we approached life as a game. We may have cried and struggled, but we never turned to harmful coping mechanisms. Instead, we persevered and emerged stronger.

Contrary to popular belief, a cigarette will not change your life. The temporary relief it provides is simply an illusion, leading to a dangerous cycle of addiction. The real solution lies within ourselves, and the choices we make. Shouldn't we strive to be a shining example for others, setting an example of what is right and wrong? If we cannot change our own small habits and become better versions of ourselves, how can we hope to inspire and make a positive impact on the world? Let us take small actions, such as protecting our health, and strive to be a source of inspiration for all.

Dear reader, Have you ever thought about the impact your actions have on those around you? We all have a responsibility to not only take care of ourselves, but to also help those in need. People tell me to stop judging people based on superficial things like smoking or drinking. While it's true that these habits may not define someone's character, they can still have a negative effect on those around them.

It's crucial to call people out on their harmful behavior and let them know that they are doing wrong. Think about all the money you spend on cigarettes or alcohol. Instead of letting it go to waste, why not use it to help others in need? The feeling of generosity and kindness will last a lifetime and bring you a sense of joy and happiness that can never be replicated.

So the next time you're feeling stressed or overwhelmed, don't reach for that bottle of alcohol. Instead, Do what I always do when I'm stressed, take a moment to help someone in need. The smile on their face will be all the reward you need. Remember, we all have a responsibility to make the world a better place. Let's start by helping each other and spreading kindness wherever we go Is this a big step? No right. But I hope you can see how many lives it can change. Firstly, It changes your life by making you happy and keeping you healthy by preventing you from smoking or drinking. Secondly, it helps the poor. Thirdly, it inspires people around you to do the same and thereby creating a chain which will bring a change. This is the purpose of this book.

Dear reader, Smartphones have become a major part of our lives, but they can also be a source of addiction and distraction. Many of us don't realize the extent of our dependence on our phones until we check our daily screen-time. Despite being busy with work, study, or other activities, most people still spend over five hours on their screens every day.

It's a sad reality that we often prioritize our phones over the people we love. We tell our kids we're too busy to spend time with them, and we ignore the pleas of our elderly parents. We also dodge calls from friends, claiming we're too busy, when in reality we're just distracted by our screens.

It's time to ask ourselves a crucial question - are we really too busy, or are we lying to ourselves and the world? To find out, take a moment to check your digital well-being on your phone. This feature will show you how much time you spend on your phone and which apps you use the most. Once you have this information, it's up to you to decide if you're truly busy, or if you're just letting your phone control your life.

There are so many such things which we do and not realize they are wrong. To make you realize and to show you what is right and wrong and how you can do the right things, How you can take small things and create a difference in your life, I have given this most valuable knowledge which I understood and realized at a very young age. To correct our lives and to not just tell things or motivate you like everyone does I have written this book. This book is not a motivation, It's a complete guide. Complete stepwise process to bring change and to actually fulfil "**the purpose of Life**"

1. Meditation

We are four of us in family. My dad, mom, my brother and me and now even you "the reader" is a part of my small family and that is why I want to help you to lead a life in better way. I realized what is good and bad after going through a lot of things and problems. But I want to tell you and give you a shortcut so that you don't pass through all of it. I want to tell you everything wrong that I did and realized it and help you early and stop you from doing those mistakes So that you can achieve everything faster and not waste your precious life years. I want you to be the change. A change that will create a better you and a better world.

We had lot of problems in our family and as a kid I saw a lot of things. I will try to tell you as many stories as I can and share my life with you so that you don't get bored. So since we had a lot of problems I tried various jobs at a very early age. Until finally I became a teacher.

As a teacher I meet lot of students and interact with them. I see lot of my students and everyone facing one issue that is not being able to focus for long or concentrate. And short video content on the Internet (reels, shorts etc.) has worsened it more. Once upon a time people used to read books and newspapers, then the shift took place to radio where people started hearing things for hours.

Then the television arrived and people used to sit for hours and watch series and movies. Each movie used to be 3 hours. Then slowly the length of the movies began to reduce. Then people started watching things on Internet. They started watching short films and then they started seeing content in 10 minutes video form. The length of videos began to reduce and today it's just 15sec. People watch 15 second videos and want all the knowledge and information in 15 seconds. This process led to reduction of human attention span. We don't realize how our attention time has reduced. We cannot sit for hours and watch a movie. We start getting bored if a movie is long. We want instant entertainment. We want everything instantly. Then how can you Imagine to sit for hours and read the book and learn for your exams. So, what can be done?

If you see on the internet, you'll find people giving nonsense ideas and solutions. These people say things like, a human can focus only 40 minutes. They say take breaks and so on. But I'm completely against this idea. We should not underestimate human abilities. I read books sometimes whole day and don't realize the time passing. I can complete two books in a day. But, nowadays only thing people are interested is, their phones. To avoid this and to develop good concentration powers I suggest everyone to do meditation.

It is a very underrated thing. We have not realized the power of meditation. So, are you interested to know about how it helped me and how it still does?

Once I completed my school entered college I was distracted from my goals. I saw life as a means of enjoyment. But things changed as I realized what I'm doing with my life. Is life only about me?? I questioned myself and then material things stopped making me happy. I became goal oriented and wanted to help the world and prevent them from doing wrong things. But to do this I needed to be an intelligent person and intelligence comes from reading books. But I could not sit and read without getting distracted.

So, I decided to try meditation to help me learn to focus and concentrate. But whenever I sat to meditate lot of thought good, bad, ugly, dirty came to my mind. I was frustrated and lost hope but then Instead of quitting like everyone does, I decided to learn about it. But sadly, there was not much content about meditation but still I decided to go with whatever I found.

I found people telling that you shouldn't worry about thoughts. Thoughts come and go, Just embrace them, Don't try to ignore them. Once I did that while meditating after few minutes my mind started to get blank, Because I focused on every thought my mind wouldn't have anything more to distract me.

Then I started to focus on the middle of my head and concentrate on my breathing. This also helped me breathe better and made me energetic. When you do things consciously body accepts it better. When you breathe consciously oxygen is better absorbed and you can feel the effect. But all of these is secondary, Slowly with time I learned to focus and concentrate. I practised to sit at one place for hours without getting distracted. I learned to give time to myself.

Aren't these the qualities that you need to become good reader??

You must be able to focus on book, You must be able to sit for hours and not get tired or bored. This is what you achieve with meditation.

What if I don't want to read??

Will meditation still help me?

Yes, Every one of us have so many thoughts in our head running always. It doesn't let us be productive and focused. All of us face so many problem and we don't know how to react and handle them.

People smoke and drink because they think smoking and drinking relieves them from stress. Once the effect of it is over, they drink and smoke again and thus depend on these harmful things making them their habit. But when you meditate you learn to control your thoughts. Your thoughts don't haunt you. Stress is no more a thing. Depression is no more a problem if you learn to let it go.

Ancient people had bigger problems than what we face today. People lost their lives, family and had so may issues that you and I cannot even think of, but did you see any depressed king? any depressed queen? and today depression is a fashion, everyone proudly says they are depressed. But why?

Depression is in our control. If you learn to manage small stress in its initial stages it doesn't reach to a level of depression. As a young child, I had experienced such pain and turmoil before. I watched as the two people I loved the most, my parents, fought in front of my eyes. I was just in 6th standard, and the events that transpired left an indelible mark on my young mind. I watched in horror as my parents fought, and one even attempted suicide. Despite witnessing such traumatic events, I never gave in to depression. I stood strong even as everything around me seemed to crumble.

I was young and innocent, but I knew deep down that I had to be strong for myself and my family. I saw everything that was dear to me falling apart, but I refused to let it break me. I learned that we often underestimate our own strength and overestimate the power of our problems.

As you read my story, I know that you may feel emotional and sad, imagining the hardships that I had to endure as a child. But that's the thing - we tend to get overwhelmed by our problems, and feel like we are the only ones facing such difficulties. We question why our lives are so hard, and why we have to go through such pain. But that's exactly what I want to emphasize - we must never let our problems define us. We must not break down and give in to despair.

We must look within ourselves and find the strength to overcome any obstacle that comes our way. We must remember that we are not alone in our struggles, and that we have the power to rise above it all. I may have been just a child when my parents fought, but I was able to survive the trauma and emerge stronger. I want to inspire others to do the same, and show that no matter what life throws at us, we have the power to overcome it and thrive.

But one question no one asks when they are stressed is-

"If I can do nothing about it, why should I worry about it?"

I know I will sound harsh now but a problem as small as break up or as huge as a death isn't abnormal. Things happen. People die, people fall sick, people lose money, people become poor. Anything can happen. Can you stop it?

If you can then definitely you should. If I could solve the issues between my parents I definitely would. But if I, couldn't I should accept it and shouldn't think about it.

If you are a doctor and treat patients and get emotional about them, can you treat them?? can you do operations without your hands shaking?

Similarly, if you need to solve a problem you must not get affected by it.

And here comes the power of meditation, It helps you to learn to see the truth as it is, without being affected or without getting distracted with unwanted thoughts like what will I do, What how will I survive after breakup.

You'll be able to learn to live in the present and take right action.

Let me tell you the uses of meditation:

Stress reduction through meditation is a well-established benefit. Stress is a normal part of life, but chronic stress can have negative effects on our physical and mental health. Meditation has been shown to help reduce stress by changing our physiological and psychological responses to stress.

As a young boy, I was inspired by the power of medicine and the healing touch of a doctor. I wanted to help those in need, to bring comfort and hope to those who felt hopeless. My passion for helping others drove me to pursue a career in medicine. However, my dreams were shattered when I was unable to clear my medical entrance examination.

Despite my dedication and hard work, I found myself lost and discouraged. I had joined a coaching institute that proved to be a waste of time and resources, and I felt like I had lost a precious year of my life. But I did not give up. I took charge of my own education, studying at home and scoring well in Physics and Biology. Though I struggled with Chemistry, I was still able to secure a seat in a pharmacy college.

However, studying pharmacy was not what I had envisioned for myself. I yearned to continue my journey to become a doctor, but If I cleared the NEET, I had to leave the college I was studying in and pay entire 4-year fees even if I hadn't completed my education of

Pharmacy, financial constraints and rules made it impossible for me to do so. My heart was heavy and I felt like I was simply going through stress, but I found solace in meditation. It helped me cope with my stress and brought clarity to my thoughts. I realized that I could still make a difference in people's lives, even if it wasn't through my personal journey as a doctor.

I found purpose in teaching and motivating others. I taught my students for the NEET exam and encouraged them to pursue their own dreams of becoming a doctor. And now, as I see my students succeed, I am filled with pride and joy. I may not have become the doctor I dreamed of, but I am still making a positive impact on the world, and that is what truly matters.

But how does meditation help?

Physiologically, meditation can lower the levels of the stress hormone cortisol and decrease activity in the amygdala, a region of the brain that is responsible for the body's stress response. This leads to a physical relaxation response, including lower blood pressure, slower heart rate, and reduced muscle tension.

Psychologically, meditation can help change the way we perceive stress and learn to respond to it in a more positive and calm manner. It can help us develop a more accepting and non-judgmental attitude towards stress and increase our ability to manage and cope with it.

In addition, mindfulness meditation, in particular, can help individuals develop a greater awareness of their thoughts and emotions, and thus gain better control over their reactions to stress. By focusing on the present moment and letting go of worries and concerns, individuals can become more resilient to stress and its effects.

Stress reduction through meditation is a beneficial aspect of incorporating meditation into daily life. Regular meditation practice can help individuals develop a more relaxed and calm response to stress, leading to improved physical and mental well-being.

A. **Focus and concentration**-Meditation can help improve focus and concentration by training the mind to be more present and attentive. The act of focusing the mind during meditation can increase cognitive control and the ability to sustain attention, leading to improved focus and concentration in daily life.

So when I couldn't clear my exam how did I reach a state where I mastered the subject and started teaching others and helping them. How did I start teaching others and helping them become doctors?

Meditation helped me improve my focus and concentration despite lot going on around me. I Started studying again along with my Pharmacy syllabus. Initially it was difficult to manage both but finally as my concentration improved, I could study both and reached a state where I could help others to learn. But did meditation really help me? How does it help improve concentration and focus?

Meditation can increase activity in the prefrontal cortex, a part of the brain that is involved in executive functions such as attention and working memory. By strengthening this part of the brain, meditation can help individuals maintain focus and concentrate better in demanding and challenging situations.

In addition, mindfulness meditation, in particular, can help individuals become more aware of distractions and increase their ability to redirect their attention back to the task at hand. By learning to let go of thoughts and distractions during meditation, individuals can apply this skill to daily life, resulting in better focus and concentration.

Incorporating meditation into daily life can help improve focus and concentration by training the mind to be more present and attentive, and by strengthening the brain's ability to maintain focus and attention. Regular meditation practice can lead to better productivity and performance, both in personal and professional life.

B. **Positive impact on empathy and compassion** by changing the way individuals perceive and respond to others. Empathy is the ability to understand and share the feelings of others, while compassion is the desire to alleviate the suffering of others.

Research has shown that regular meditation practice can increase activity in regions of the brain that are associated with empathy and compassion, such as the anterior cingulate cortex and the insula.

This increased activity can lead to greater awareness and understanding of the emotions and experiences of others.

Mindfulness meditation, in particular, can help individuals develop a more non-judgmental and accepting attitude towards themselves and others. By becoming more aware of their own thoughts, emotions, and behaviors, individuals can gain a deeper understanding of their own experiences and apply this to their interactions with others. This increased self-awareness can lead to greater empathy and compassion for others.

In addition, compassion, focused meditation can help individuals cultivate a more compassionate attitude towards themselves and others. Through specific techniques such as visualization and affirmations, individuals can develop a deeper sense of compassion and desire to help others.

Meditation can also help individuals develop greater empathy and compassion by increasing awareness and understanding of the experiences of others, and by cultivating a more compassionate attitude towards themselves and others. This can lead to better relationships and a more harmonious world.

Improves physical health too,

a) Reducing pain: Meditation has been shown to have a positive impact on reducing pain. By focusing the mind on the present moment, individuals can decrease their perception of pain and reduce activity in the pain centers of the brain. This can lead to reduced discomfort and improved physical well-being.

b) Lowering blood pressure: Regular meditation has been shown to lower blood pressure, which is a risk factor for heart disease and stroke. By reducing stress and promoting relaxation, meditation can lower blood pressure and improve cardiovascular health.

c) Improving sleep: Meditation has been shown to improve sleep quality by reducing stress and anxiety, which are common causes of sleep problems.

One of my friend told me that he finds it difficult to sleep in the night. Even if he closes his eyes and lays down on the bed, He doesn't get sleep for hours. Lots of thoughts come to his mind and he keeps thinking of them. He used to start worrying about his career and his future whenever he went to sleep. He was worried about future which did not let him sleep. I suggested him to meditation and that has improved his sleep significantly. But how did it help?

By training the mind to be calm and relaxed, individuals can fall asleep more easily and sleep more deeply, leading to improved physical and mental well-being. Meditation makes the mind calm and relaxed. But what about people who want to sleep less and yet be productive.

I was once employed at a well-known pizza company where my primary role was delivering piping hot pizzas to eager customers. During my time at pharmacy college, I had to bid farewell to my previous job where I was delivering milk, due to its conflicting schedule with my studies. I took up this night-shift pizza delivery job as a means of supporting myself financially, despite the challenges it presented. Working late into the night, I found it difficult to get a proper amount of sleep, but I refused to let this hinder my success.

It was through the practice of meditation that I was able to overcome this obstacle and maintain my energy levels, even with limited rest. If you're someone who feels like they're sleeping too much, meditation could be the solution you've been searching for. Not only does it allow you to reduce your sleep quota, but it also helps in boosting energy levels, which is essential for a busy, fast-paced life.

a) Decreasing inflammation: Inflammation is linked to many chronic diseases such as heart disease, diabetes, and cancer. Meditation has been shown to decrease inflammation by reducing stress and promoting relaxation, leading to improved physical health.

b) Boosting the immune system: Regular meditation has been shown to improve the functioning of the immune system, helping to fight off illness and disease. I have a very good immunity and I think the reason might be meditation. I cannot tell this with full surety because I did not feel it happen only after doing meditation, but When I got COVID I recovered from it in just few days. I used to drink Khada in the night, which is a medicine prepared using cloves, cinnamon, honey etc. and also continued my meditation. I never fall sick often. So if you follow my book and do everything I say and follow my check-sheet You will surely see a positive impact on your health.

How meditation improves immunity may be because By reducing stress and promoting relaxation, it can help the immune system function more effectively, leading to improved physical health.

Other benefits

a) Increased self-awareness: Meditation can help increase self-awareness and promote a deeper understanding of one's thoughts, emotions and behaviors. I always know what goes inside me and that is the reason why I always control my reactions. I react very less to situations and practised to stay calm. I don't get angry soon at small things and don't get hurt easily. All thanks to meditation which helped me observe what goes inside me. If you learn to understand yourself you can learn to change yourself. I never get addicted to anything because I realize it early when I start depending on things. Most people struggle with understanding themselves and that's why they don't realize when they get addicted to things and at last the addiction becomes so strong that they can't leave it.

My journey towards self-awareness and breaking free from harmful habits began with my recognition of my excessive use of social media. I was shocked to realize that I was spending countless hours scrolling through my feeds and interacting with virtual friends, while neglecting my real-life relationships and responsibilities. I made the decision to delete all of my social media accounts, except for YouTube, which I used as a platform to educate and inspire others.

Next, I tackled my unhealthy addiction to pani puri. The spicy, crunchy street food had become a staple in my diet, and I was consuming it nearly every day. But I soon realized the dangers of consuming so much of it and decided to limit my intake to rare occasions.

My journey towards a healthier lifestyle continued when I started going to the gym and incorporating black coffee into my diet as a pre-workout boost. However, before long, I was drinking coffee even in the evenings and during my college breaks. I soon realized that I was becoming dependent on caffeine, and didn't want to be held captive by any substance. So, I made the difficult decision to quit coffee and tea altogether, and have been caffeine-free for years now.

These experiences taught me the importance of self-awareness and taking control of my habits. I learned that it's never too late to change and break free from harmful addictions, and that meditation can be a powerful tool for achieving self-awareness and inner peace.

b) Enhanced creativity and productivity: Regular meditation can lead to increased creativity, problem-solving skills and productivity.

So, I think now it is clear to you how Meditation is very important.

I do it every day when I wake up after brushing. It's the first thing that I do when I wake up. Start with 10 minutes of meditation. You can find guided meditation apps or on YouTube which will help you to start your journey but as you become good, please stop depending on those. I personally prefer Mantra meditation, but you can also simply focus on breathing and do it without chanting too.

2. Bhagavad gita

Bhagavad gita is another thing which changed my life a lot.

When I was at school the first thing that we did after entering school was prayer and our prayer consisted of Bhagavad gita chapters. They did not tell us the meanings of the verses, But just made us chant them.

But later When I entered college and did not have a beautiful life. I questioned myself. I questioned myself what is it that has changed?

Why am I not as happy as I used to be?

But then I found the answer. Bhagavad gita. Though i didn't know the meaning, My days went beautiful because of the tone, Because that brought an harmony. I think the start of your day decided how well your day will be? Agree? If your day starts beautiful it ends well too.

But my days could never start beautiful. Growing up in a household filled with constant fights and chaos had a profound impact on me. My mornings were filled with the sounds of angry voices and shattered glass. I remember waking up to find everything in my home in disarray and stepping on broken pieces of glass on the floor. But amidst all the chaos, I found solace in one thing - the sound of the verses from the Bhagavad Gita. Every day, before I headed off to school, I would immerse myself in the peace and wisdom of this ancient text. It was a way for me to forget the turmoil I faced at home and feel centered and calm. This is why the Bhagavad Gita holds a special place in my heart. It has been my refuge and source of comfort through all the difficulties of my childhood and continues to be an important part of my life today.

So, when I entered college again my life changed, when i began to feel lonely and unhappy in college, I decided to rediscover the peace and happiness that I had experienced as a child, and the Bhagavad gita became my guide once again. I began to recite the verses every morning and night. But this time with a change, I started to read the meaning too, and I started to notice a change in my perspective and my outlook on life. The struggles and challenges that I faced in college no longer seemed insurmountable, and I was filled with a renewed sense of purpose and direction. The power of the gita was not just in its teachings, but in the way it brought me closer to my true self. I felt like I was reclaiming the child who had been through so much and emerged unscathed, and I knew that I was capable of facing anything that came my way. The Bhagavad gita had a transformative impact on my life, and I am eternally grateful for its teachings.

Every question that anyone can ask is already asked by Arjuna in the Gita and every solution that we want is already given by Krishna. If this is not enough then let me tell you advantages of reading bhagavad gita.

Here are some of the advantages of reading the Bhagavad Gita in personal life:

Increased wisdom: The Bhagavad Gita is rich in spiritual teachings and offers a wealth of wisdom and insights into the nature of reality and the human condition. Reading the text can help individuals gain a deeper understanding of themselves and the world around them.

Growing up, I always felt a strong sense of responsibility towards helping others. Whether it was a friend in need or a stranger on the street, I have always felt compelled to offer a helping hand. So, when my friends started coming to me with their problems and seeking advice, I saw it as an opportunity to fulfill my lifelong goal of being a support system for others.

I believe that it's important to be there for people when they need it the most, especially in today's fast-paced world where everyone is so focused on their own problems and worries. My mission is to make sure that everyone who comes to me goes back feeling better, even if just a little bit. I understand that I am not perfect and may not always have the perfect solution, but I always strive to make sure that my words of wisdom and comfort bring a smile to their face.

As a listener, I strive to not judge those who come to me, but instead, I try to understand their situation and offer a kind and non-judgmental ear. It's important to remember that everyone is fighting their own battles and we should all strive to be a source of comfort and support for those in need. And, if we can do that, we will have truly fulfilled our purpose of being there for others. But to act properly and to be able to talk properly we need wisdom and for me Bhagavad gita was a major source of wisdom and knowledge.

Wisdom is an ability to act productively using knowledge, experience, common sense. It is ability to decide what is right and wrong and take the right actions. So, we need to learn to react correctly in situations and we should learn to respond in the right way. so, to achieve all of these reading Bhagavad gita becomes important.

Improved mental clarity: The teachings of the Bhagavad Gita encourage individuals to think critically and reflect on the nature of their thoughts and actions. This can lead to increased mental clarity and a greater understanding of one's own thoughts and behaviors.

Like many times in my life, I had to take very important decisions. I had to decide what to do with my life. These decisions can either destroy or improve the life. So how to have a mental clarity? How to be able to stay clear with the mind. Lot of people are confused and don't have a clarity with their thought and to solve it Bhagavad gita is the best solution.

Krishna gives Arjuna mental clarity in this book. Arjuna was a person who was just like us. He had to fight his own family members. His own family members were standing against him to kill him and he was confused. It happens to lot of us. Many times, our parents forcefully make us do what we don't like. They make to to take a course which we don't like and make us to learn something and get a job which we would never be happy with. Dear reader, they are not wrong either but they think and decide our future based on their past and their experience. They want us to be happy but they may be wrong sometimes since the world is changing. But how to take the right decision. Should I fight with them and do what I like? Same confusion Arjuna had. He was confused and didn't want to fight against his own family. He told Krishna that how can I fight against my own family. I can never be happy killing them. Krishna guides him and tells him what is right and wrong. All of us need such a teacher and guide who will help us to take right decision. So why not become Arjuna and make Krishna our guide and a teacher.

Enhanced spirituality: The Bhagavad Gita is a spiritual text that teaches about the nature of the soul and the ultimate purpose of human existence. Reading the text can deepen an individual's connection to spirituality and promote personal growth and self-discovery.

I'm not very spiritual either but I understand the value of spirituality. Spirituality is about understanding being normal human beings. It's about the nature of the soul and the purpose of the life. It allows us to make the best use of our life. So, if you are interested in spirituality too Bhagavad gita is a book to go with.

Greater inner peace: The Bhagavad Gita teaches about the importance of detachment and the role of actions in achieving inner peace. By practicing these teachings, individuals can experience greater inner peace and reduced stress and anxiety.

Inner peace is one of the most important things. In a world where depression is increasing managing stress is very important. One of my teacher explained me how depression starts and what depression is. As a young student in my pharmacy college, I was fortunate enough to have a truly remarkable teacher. He was an exceptional educator who made every lesson enjoyable and memorable. His teaching style was unique and captivating, and I quickly fell in love with teaching as a result of his influence. When he would walk into the classroom, he would first take a few minutes to write the important points of the lesson on the board, once he was finished writing, the atmosphere would shift and the room would be filled with pin-drop silence. The students were so focused and attentive, eagerly soaking in every word that he said. He would not even allow us to take notes or touch our pens, as he did not want us to be even a single percent distracted. Under his guidance, I was able to grasp the material with ease and clarity, and I knew I would never forget his lessons.

I could understand everything he taught. In one class he told us that how depression happens and what it was. He told us that depression occurs when a person is stressed. But there is a difference. Stress is initial stage of depression. If you learn to manage stress early It does not turn in to depression. Depression happens when a person keeps thinking of one thing and when he is constantly in stress and because of which stress hormones are released and this also damages his physical health.

So dear reader, Little bit of stress is not a bad thing, all of us have it. It helps us to take action. But not being able to control it early and not being able to manage it is a big problem. It becomes a problem when you are constantly at stress and don't find inner peace. That is another reason you must start reading Bhagavad gita

Improved ethics: The Bhagavad Gita teaches about the importance of ethics and morality in leading a fulfilling life. By incorporating these teachings into daily life, individuals can improve their own ethical behavior and become better role models for others.

Gita plays a major role in who I am today and how I handle problems today. Because of that I also made a YouTube channel where I began to upload gita videos daily so that people spend time in Gita too. I wanted people to do something important other than seeing 15 second dance videos of girls on the Internet. Since I consider the reader reading this as a family, I suggest you to please try reading Gita for a week. I have added it in the check-sheet. Please manage to read it for 7 days and see the difference yourself because,

"Some things cannot be told, They need to be felt."

3. Exercise

I am very sure you might have heard of all these things that I told until now. There have been people who might have suggested you. But why don't we take action??

Because we don't have a solid plan and motivation.

Let me first share with you how exercise helped me.

In school I was a student who studied well. I was focused more on studies because of the problems in my family. But everyone has problem with first benchers. Everyone thinks they are weak and try to take advantage of them. Back benchers always find ways to irritate them and make fun of them.

When I was a child, something strange began to form in my hand. At first, it appeared greenish in color and I was deeply concerned. I sought advice from multiple doctors, but they dismissed my concerns, telling me that it was simply a green appearance caused by veins. Despite their reassurances, I could feel the pain whenever I wrote for a longer period or engaged in any physical activity. The discomfort was real and scary, but I felt unheard and alone as the doctors continued to deny my experiences.

By the time I reached 9th grade, the situation had become worse. The tumour had grown and the pain had become extreme. I was unable to do the things that brought me joy. The fear and frustration of not being understood by those who were supposed to help me only added to my pain. The experience was a dark and emotional journey, one that left me feeling vulnerable and helpless.

Despite the constant pain I was experiencing, I was determined to continue my training in karate. Every punch I threw was like a sharp stab, but I refused to let the pain stop me. I was a fighter at heart and nothing was going to get in the way of that. Every time I stepped into a fight to defend myself from people, I felt a surge of adrenaline and a fierce determination to succeed. I refused to let anyone take advantage of me and I stood up against injustice whenever I saw it.

I was not only fighting for myself, but also for others. I had friends who were being teased and bullied, and I was determined to be there for them. I used the skills I had learned in karate to protect and defend those who were in need. Every victory I achieved, no matter how small, filled me with a sense of pride and accomplishment.

Despite the challenges I faced, I never gave up on my dreams. I was determined to push through the pain and become the best karate fighter I could be. My unwavering spirit and my unwavering commitment to what was right inspired others and brought hope to those who needed it most. To this day, I am proud of the fighter I became and the impact I made on those around me.

But, As a first-bencher, I often found myself alone and without a large group of friends. This isolation made me an easy target for others who were part of a group and took advantage of my loneliness.

Despite the odds stacked against me, I never backed down from a fight. I took on my opponents like a one-man army, determined to prove my worth and stand up for what was right.

The battles I fought were not just physical, but emotional as well. Every time I stepped into the fray, I felt a rush of adrenaline and a sense of bravery. I felt like a movie hero, taking on the world and standing up for what was right. In those moments, I was filled with a sense of power and a deep sense of pride in who I was and what I stood for.

I held my head high and continued to fight, never once giving up or backing down. I was determined to be true to myself, even if that meant standing alone. Today, I am proud of the person I became and the battles I fought. I may have been a lone fighter, but I never wavered in my determination and I never let anyone dim my spirit.

Still today I don't make much friends and love to be alone. But all this had one disadvantage, As a brave and independent person, I never cared about those who wanted respect for no reason. They saw my loneliness as a sign of weakness and repeatedly attacked me at my weakest point - my hand. I don't blame them for their actions, as they may have been unintentional, but their constant need to assert their superiority over front-benchers was something I could not tolerate. They had the support of their gang, which only made them feel more entitled to respect, but I refused to bow down to their bullying tactics.

Despite the pain I felt, I stood my ground and fought back. I refused to let their insults and jabs affect me. I was determined to show them that I was not weak, but strong and resilient. I took on their attacks with courage and stood firm in my beliefs, no matter how much it hurt.

Today, I look back on those battles with pride and a sense of accomplishment. I may not have had a gang to support me, but I had something far more valuable - my own strength, resilience, and unwavering spirit. And those are the traits that will always make me proud of who I am and what I stand for.

Finally, in 9th standard, I underwent surgery to treat an issue with my hand. Despite the doctor's warning that the problem may return, I held onto hope. Unfortunately, my worst fears were realized when the issue returned. The thing that broke my heart the most was the fact that I had to give up on karate, a sport that I was deeply passionate about. The thought of not being able to continue on my journey to the final belt was devastating. My love for karate was not just about the physical activity, but it was about the discipline, the focus, and the sense of achievement it brought to my life. The surgery took all of that away from me. This is the reason I could not go up to the last belt.

If you are wondering which belt, I am then I would like to tell you It's brown.

Being physically fit has taught me the value of fitness in our lives. Growing up, I was a first-bench student, but it was my passion for karate and exercise that earned me respect and the confidence to stand up for what is right. I strongly believe that health and fitness play a crucial role in our ability to bring about change and make a positive impact on the world around us. To be able to take on the challenges and obstacles that come our way, we need to have the energy and strength that can only come from regular exercise.

As a result, I would like to offer the following advice to you dear reader: if you want to make a difference, prioritize your physical well-being by making exercise a habit. Whether you participate in a sport, go to the gym, or simply go for a walk or run, the key is to find an activity that you enjoy and stick to it regularly. Not only will you feel better and more energetic, but you will also be equipping yourself with the tools you need to tackle any obstacle that comes your way.

In conclusion, the benefits of exercise are countless, both for our personal growth and for the betterment of society. So, dear reader, I implore you to make exercise a priority in your life and never underestimate the power of being fit and healthy.

Here are some advantages of exercise:

A. **Improved physical health**: Exercise helps to improve cardiovascular health, build muscle and strength, and maintain a healthy weight. It can also reduce the risk of chronic diseases such as heart disease, stroke, and type 2 diabetes. Regular exercise also helps to improve posture, flexibility, and balance.

Nowadays, India is called Diabetes capital of world. Do you want to give India this name permanently or do you want to be healthy. Diabetes is a serious problem which can be controlled at an early age. You can prevent it at an early stage by exercise. So, if the story I told you about me is not enough to give you a strong reason to exercise then hope this reason does.

B. **Increased energy and focus**: Exercise helps to boost energy levels by increasing blood flow and oxygen to the brain. It also releases endorphins, which are feel-good hormones that help to reduce stress and anxiety. Exercise can also improve focus and concentration by promoting the growth of new brain cells and improving brain function.

C. **Better mental health**: Exercise has been shown to have a positive impact on mental health. Regular exercise can help to reduce symptoms of depression and anxiety and improve overall mood. Exercise can also increase self-esteem and confidence and promote a sense of well-being.

D. **Improved sleep:** Regular exercise has been shown to improve the quality of sleep, making it easier to fall asleep and stay asleep. This leads to increased energy and improved mood during the day.

E. **Weight management:** Exercise can help to maintain a healthy weight by burning calories and building muscle. This can also lead to improved body composition and a greater sense of body confidence.

You might be thinking If exercise is so important why didn't I place it at the beginning. I did not place it at the beginning because though it is important it is not as important as Meditation and Bhagavad gita. Mind comes first, then comes body. Mental health is more important. If i was not mentally strong and determined My physical fitness could never help me tackle group of people.

I started going to gym at an early age because I always knew the value of health. I agree you can walk; you can do basic exercises at home and don't require a gym. But I needed an environment. Gym gave me an environment which took away my laziness and kept me motivated to exercise. At home there will be days when you feel lazy and skip exercise but if you pay money for gym, you will want to go and not waste your money. You will also see other people working out and exercising which will make you work harder.

Breathing Exercise

But one of the most critical forms of exercise that is often overlooked is breathing exercise. In our world today, with increasing levels of pollution, it is imperative to prioritize our lung health. That's why setting aside time each morning to engage in breathing exercises is so crucial. By strengthening our lungs through regular practice, we can build our respiratory system's resilience, ensuring we are able to breathe clean air and live a healthy life.

Breathing exercises not only improve lung function, but they also have a range of benefits for overall health. They can help reduce stress, improve focus and concentration, boost energy levels, and increase feelings of calm and relaxation. It's a simple, yet effective way to prioritize our health and well-being, and it can be done anywhere, at any time, making it an accessible and convenient form of exercise for everyone.

So, I encourage you to make breathing exercises a regular part of your routine. Whether it's five minutes in the morning, or ten minutes before bed, set aside some time to focus on your breath and give your lungs the attention they deserve. By taking care of our respiratory health, we can lay the foundation for a lifetime of good health and well-being.

So dear reader, even If you ignore all the advice I gave about physical exercise please don't skip this. Please add it in your life. Breathing exercises are very important. If you have a question on how to do it. So here is how you do it-

a) Ujjayi Breath: Ujjayi breath is a smooth, slow and continuous breath where you exhale and inhale through the nose while making a soft, gentle "ocean" sound. To do this, close your mouth and slightly constrict the back of your throat as if you were trying to fog up a mirror.

Instructions:

Begin by sitting comfortably in a seated position with a straight back and your chin slightly tucked in.

Breathe in deeply through your nose, and then exhale out through your mouth with a soft hissing sound, similar to the sound of the ocean.

Repeat this breathing pattern for several breaths, feeling your abdomen expand and contract with each inhale and exhale.

Keep your focus on the sound and sensation of the breath.

b) Nadi Shodhana: Nadi Shodhana, also known as Alternate Nostril Breathing, is a simple yet powerful breathing technique that helps calm the mind and balance the nervous system.

Instructions:

Sit comfortably in a seated position with a straight back and your chin slightly tucked in.

Using your right hand, place your index and middle finger between your eyebrows.

Place your thumb on your right nostril and your ring and pinky finger on your left nostril.

Close your right nostril with your thumb and inhale deeply through your left nostril.

Then close your left nostril with your fingers and release your right nostril, exhaling through it.

Inhale through the right nostril, then close it and exhale through the left nostril.

Continue alternating sides with each inhale and exhale for several breaths.

c) Kapalabhati Breath: Kapalabhati breath is a strong, invigorating breathing technique that helps to cleanse the lungs and stimulate the digestive system.

Instructions:

Sit comfortably in a seated position with a straight back and your chin slightly tucked in.

Begin by taking a few deep breaths in and out through your nose.

Exhale with force, contracting your abdominal muscles to push the air out of your lungs.

Inhale passively, allowing the air to flow back into your lungs as your abdominal muscles relax.

Repeat this rapid inhale-exhale pattern for several breaths, focusing on the contraction and release of your abdominal muscles

Remember dear reader, when you are doing these breathing exercises, it's important to be comfortable and relaxed. Start with a few breaths and gradually increase as you feel more comfortable. It's also helpful to incorporate these breathing techniques into your daily routine.

"Every time someone makes a wish,

They do it for themself whilst being selfish"

4. A story of a beautiful girl

Once upon a time, I was running late for college in my 11th standard. As I approached the college gates, I was stopped and denied entry for being late. But instead of sitting there feeling bored, I turned to my trusty bag of magic tricks and began entertaining the other students who had been similarly delayed.

It was then that a group of commerce students approached me, among them was a stunning and beautiful girl. I felt an immediate spark as I took her hand to perform a card trick. There was something different about her, an aura of innocence that set her apart from the others. I was struck by an intense desire to get her number. But how could I make that happen? I was determined to find a way. The encounter marked the start of a journey filled with wonder, uncertainty, and a growing sense of connection.

Then I decided I wanted to get her number and talk to her. But how?

I was neither bold enough to directly ask for her number, nor did I believe she was the type of girl who would readily hand it over to a stranger. So, I thought of an idea. I suggested to the group that we all exchange numbers and become friends. This way, my request wouldn't seem out of place or awkward. It worked and I finally got everyone's numbers. And you know what I did immediately after that meet?

I deleted everyone's number except this girl.

I went home and texted her 'Hii' and i got no reply but she was online. Then I waited and texted her "What are you doing?" and still got no reply. Then I thought I will never get her reply and will be ignored. But then I thought if I have to be ignored anyways and If I'm anyways going to lose her why should I keep quiet. She anyways had insulted me by not replying to me so I scolded her. I scolded her telling that "What do you think of yourself? If you don't want to reply, at least tell that you don't want to talk." and then finally I got her reply.

And then conversations went smoothly and we spoke for hours.

But whenever I saw her in college, I couldn't talk to her. I was consumed by a deep sense of shyness and fear. Even now, the reasons for my anxiety remain shrouded in mystery. Every day, I regret not gathering the courage to speak with her on subsequent encounters. I could easily converse with her through text messages, but in person, I found myself tongue-tied and frozen. Every time I caught a glimpse of her, I was overcome with fear and would quickly turn and flee, not daring to engage in conversation. To my surprise, she felt just as scared as I did, and we spent our time at college barely acknowledging each other's existence.

But that one missed opportunity still haunts me to this day. Every time I think about it, I feel a pang of regret in my heart, knowing that I could have made a lasting memory with her on that graduation day. She looked so stunning in her saree, with a radiance that lit up the place. Yet, I was too timid and scared to even capture a photo with her. It was as if my fear had overpowered me, and I couldn't take up the courage to seize the moment.

Looking back, every conversation with her was a lesson in the true meaning of being a good person. She was the epitome of kindness, honesty, hard work, strength, and consistency. Her unwavering spirit inspired me and taught me so much about how to be a better person. Even now, years after our last day in college, she remains a source of inspiration in my life. I am grateful for the impact she had on me, and I will always cherish the memories of our fleeting moments together.

I wanted to share this interesting story because it is special to me.

"This is my story,

Which remains a glory"

Improve community

Tiny tweaks with a big impact

So, what can we do to change our community. I told you how we can change our lives but how can we bring a change in the community level. So, everything that you will learn in community level also will include personal level. Because as you take actions for others, it also helps you at personal levels.

But firstly, what is community. When lot of people join together it is called as a community. Lot of communities form a society which forms a country which further forms world. So now we are ready at personal level. We have done everything that it takes to become good individual.

So why should we care about communities?

Every Human being including you "dear reader" needs help, needs some guidance to do well. If I would have been selfish and thought only about myself, could I write this book? NO right. I could write this book only because I wanted to guide people and help community.

We must think about others because we are humans. Real happiness comes from helping others.

Dear reader, Imagine, As you walked down the busy road, you suddenly heard a loud crash and turned to see a person lying motionless on the ground. Panic seized you as you realized the person had met with a terrible accident and was in a life-or-death state. You quickly pulled out your phone and dialed for an ambulance, your hands shaking with urgency.

Around you, people were busy recording the scene on their phones, their actions a sharp contrast to the gravity of the situation. But you were determined to act, to do something to save this person's life.

The ambulance arrived quickly and the person was rushed to the hospital, their fate unknown. The doctors told you that if you had arrived even a few minutes later, it would have been too late. The thought of this person dying because of your inaction was too much to bear.

But despite the fear and uncertainty, you refused to give up. And then, a miracle occurred. The person's vital signs stabilized and they were pulled back from the brink of death.

Tears of relief flooded your eyes as you realized the magnitude of what you had just accomplished. You had saved a life. This person, this stranger, would live to see another day because of your actions.

The family of the person soon arrived at the hospital, their faces a mix of gratitude and disbelief. You saw a small, young daughter clinging to her father's hand, and a newly married wife crying tears of relief. In that moment, you knew that you had changed their lives forever.

This incident would stay with you for the rest of your life. The knowledge that you had made a difference, that you had saved someone from the brink of death, would be a source of pride and happiness for years to come. And as you walked out of the hospital, the weight of what you had just done hit you with full force. You had not just saved a life, but you had given hope to a family and changed the course of their future.

Imagine the pain of his wife who has just got a daughter and had given entire life to this man, She would suffer a lot if he died. She could not lead life happily. Imagine the pain of a daughter losing her dad as soon as she is born. So, Ultimately what I want to tell is just being little different, Just doing a small thing what no one does, can bring a change in an entire family. You saved an entire family by just dialing a phone number, a phone number which is just 3 digits long, a phone call to the ambulance. And now how many people are happy? It's the person who's been saved, It's the doctor who saved the life, doctor is happy because he could save the patient, wife is happy and thankful to you, Daughter is so happy that she comes to you and thanks you with an innocent face with her eyes filled with water. This is power of small change, This is how it can bring a change to family and community.

Saved in Time:

Taking right step at right time

A similar story happened with my friend. My friend was walking down the street one day when she heard a commotion coming from a nearby alley. She quickly ran over to see what was happening and was horrified to find a young girl lying on the ground, unconscious and barely breathing.

Without a moment's hesitation, my friend scooped up the girl in her arms and ran to the nearest hospital. Time was of the essence and every second counted. She could feel the girl's heart beat slowing down with each step, and the As they rushed into the emergency room, my friend was surrounded by doctors and nurses who sprang into action. The girl was quickly hooked up to machines and my friend watched anxiously as the medical team worked tirelessly to save her life. And then, a miracle happened. The girl's vital signs stabilized and she was brought back from the brink of death. My friend was overwhelmed with emotion, tears of relief streaming down her face as she watched the young girl's eyes flutter open.

The family of the girl arrived at the hospital soon after, and the gratitude in their eyes was palpable. They hugged my friend and thanked her for her quick thinking and bravery. It was clear that the girl's life had been saved because of my friend's selfless act.

The next day, my friend came to me and told me the story, and I could see the happiness and pride shining in her eyes. It was evident that this small act of kindness had changed her life in ways she never could have imagined. The power of one person's actions to make a positive impact on someone else's life was awe-inspiring.

From that day on, my friend was a changed person. She walked with a newfound sense of purpose and confidence, and she never forgot the young girl she had saved. The memory of that day would stay with her forever, a testament to the power of small acts of kindness and how they can change our lives in big and meaningful ways So If you are ready to dive into journey to change people's life, Get ready, continue reading and start taking small steps and get ready to be the change you want to see.

Everything that you read further may seem normal but no one implement it. That's the reason why I have written down in steps how you can start implementing these things and how it can bring change.

1. Gratitude

Saying thank you, yes as it as it sounds. How often do you say thank you?

As human beings, we are all interconnected in the form of community. Our lives are intertwined with those around us in countless ways, and without their support and contributions, we would not be where we are today.

Think of all the people who play a role in your daily life, from the bus driver who takes you to your destination, to the teacher who helped shape your education, to the small shopkeeper who provides you with your daily necessities. These individuals may seem small and insignificant, but they are integral pieces of a much larger puzzle that makes up our existence.

Yet, too often we take these people for granted. We forget to thank them for their efforts and their impact on our lives. We fail to realize the value they bring to our world and the impact they have had on shaping who we are.

It is time we take a step back and truly acknowledge the importance of each and every person in our lives, no matter how small or seemingly insignificant their role may be. Without their tireless work and dedication, our world would be a much different place. Let us not forget to show gratitude and appreciation for all those who make our lives richer and more fulfilling.

Can we lead life the way it is without these people?

I tell lot of people to thank everyone especially teachers. People often say, "Why should I be thankful to my teachers? They're just doing their job and getting paid for it." But I ask, does the paycheck truly reflect the amount of effort and dedication put in by these selfless individuals? Behind the classroom doors, teachers often work long hours, grading papers and preparing lessons. Despite their hard work, they are underpaid and undervalued.

However, the true reward for a teacher is not the salary they receive, but the impact they have on their students. These dedicated educators pour their hearts and souls into shaping the next generation, inspiring curiosity and a love of learning. They are not just instructors, but also mentors, role models, and friends. They help students navigate the ups and downs of life and make a lasting impact on their lives.

So I challenge those who say "why should I be thankful?" to consider the invaluable role that teachers play in shaping our future. Without their tireless efforts, where would we be? It's time to show gratitude to these unsung heroes and acknowledge the impact they have on our lives.

It's a sad reality that many people fail to appreciate the incredible impact that teachers have on our lives. Too often, they are seen as mere employees, paid to do a job and nothing more. But the truth is, teachers are so much more than that. They are the ones who shape our minds, guide us on our journeys, and provide us with the tools we need to succeed.

They pour their hearts and souls into their work, often at great personal sacrifice, and yet they are not given the recognition they deserve. It breaks my heart to think of all the dedicated teachers who struggle just to make ends meet, despite their tireless efforts to educate and inspire the next generation.

And yet, despite the challenges they face, teachers continue to show up day after day, ready to do their best. They know that their work is important, that they have the power to change lives and shape the future. They are the unsung heroes of our communities, and it's time that we start to acknowledge and appreciate their sacrifices.

"So, to all the teachers out there, I want you to know that your hard work and dedication does not go

unnoticed. You may not be rewarded with riches or fame, but your impact on the world is immeasurable. You are the ones who light the fires of imagination and awaken the passions of young minds. You are the ones who help us see the world in a new light, and who inspire us to reach for the stars. Thank you for all that you do, and know that your efforts will never be forgotten" (Rajat sharma)

Dear reader still If you don't agree with me then think of it. Think if you never had a teacher. Without them, where would you be? Without their guidance, would you have even bothered to open a book and get into the depths of knowledge? As human beings, we need that push, that motivation to keep us going. And for many of us, that push came from our teachers, whether they were inspirational or not. Even if you had a teacher who just handed out notes and didn't bother to engage, their mere presence was enough to keep you in line. You studied and learned on your own, driven by a fear of a teacher, a fear of not living up to their expectations. The reality is, without teachers, many of us would have never found the drive to learn and grow. And that is something to be thankful for, to be cherished.

So "dear reader" if you are able to read this book and understand my emotions without even having me in front of you, it's only because of the teachers whom you didn't even want to thank. You realize the value of people late.

Are you ready to start thanking people for whatever they do for you from today?

Immediately after you start this practice you can see your life and others life change. You can see your teachers smile by yourself. A teacher teaches 100s of students, but your teacher will surely remember you for showing gratitude, For telling thank you. Teacher will feel more interested and happier to teach.

Didn't a small thank you change teachers life?

I just took teacher as an example so that you can relate. You must learn to thank the shopkeeper who sells you things. You must thank the bus conductor who issues you the ticket. You must thank everyone around you. A small thank you will make their day beautiful and make them do their work better. This can change the entire community.

So now "dear reader" thousands of book out there but you chose to read this book, so I consider you as my family and thank you with lots of love. Thank you for picking this book and reading it.

Did it make you happy? Was it easy for me to tell it? It's so easy to bring a smile and thank people.

Start it from today, If not for others do it at least for yourself, Because gratitude makes you a better person. It slowly starts to change you and make you a good person. It makes you learn to appreciate the value of things. It makes you become younger by removing the age factor, Because people think they are old and don't thank the young people, once you learn gratitude you will not think about age and will treat everyone equally. You will start to become innocent as a kid and intelligent like a old.

Do you think I will end the chapter without my story. Let me tell you the story.

Gift for life:

Kindness never forgotten

As a young boy, I took on a job delivering milk and groceries to support my family. Every morning, I would rise before the sun, at the ungodly hour of 4am, to collect the milk packets and other essentials from the warehouse of the big company I worked for. My job entailed delivering these items to apartment buildings all over the city, starting at 4 and ending by 7. Despite the early hours and physically demanding work, I persevered, driven by my love and responsibility for my family.

However, the job was not without its challenges. I faced numerous setbacks along the way, from late deliveries to punctured tires in the middle of the night, when no repair shops were open. The rain would sometimes make the roads treacherous, causing me to struggle with getting the deliveries done on time. The roads in India can be a treacherous landscape, with muddy terrain in some areas and a lack of proper infrastructure. As a milk delivery boy, I faced daily struggles while navigating these roads on my overloaded bike, carrying heavy bags of milk and groceries. Despite the weight, I had to maintain my balance while dodging potholes and avoiding near-slips. The journey was extremely tiring and exhausting, and the pay was limited, just a few thousand rupees for all the hard work and effort. But through it all, I still liked my work.

But what always hurt me were the people. Some people were so rude. If I delivered the milk at 7 or got even a little late and made it by 7:30 am, I got scolded badly. The customers would tell that why are you so late in a rude tone. That hurt me. But I never argued or explained the reason for my delay and told sorry to them with my head bent. Because I knew It's not their fault either.

Every day I delivered milk and groceries before dawn, but it seemed like no matter what, I was always met with a scolding from a disgruntled customer. However, one day, I encountered a lady who was waiting for her delivery, and I was scared expecting for the same treatment. But to my surprise, she greeted me with a warm smile and thanked me for my service.

I apologized for the delay and she immediately brushed it off, telling me how grateful she was for my work, especially during the COVID-19 pandemic. She praised my bravery and dedication, delivering essentials to the doorstep while the world was staying home.

Overwhelmed by her kindness, I was even more surprised when she offered me extra money as a token of appreciation. At first, I refused, but she insisted, and I finally accepted it, holding onto it like a precious gift. That day, I felt so happy and proud of what I was doing. I chose to keep the money as a reminder of the good in people and the difference I was making in their lives. This is the power of thank you. It may be a small thing to you, but to the person whom you tell it to, it is a big thing. And it also makes you a good person and changes the lives of others too.

After leaving my milk delivery job, I made a promise to myself to never forget the struggles of those who serve us every day. No matter how small, I always make a point to give a little extra to every delivery person and local vendor I encounter. Though it may not be a substantial amount, it is my way of showing gratitude for their hard work.

Working in that company at such a young age taught me so much about the challenges faced by those who work to provide for their families. I used to be so focused on saving every penny that I would haggle with shopkeepers without a second thought. But now, the joy on their faces when I offer them a little extra means more to me than any amount of saved money.

It is a privilege to have had this experience and to have the opportunity to give back, even in small ways. Every time I see a delivery person or vendor, I am reminded of the sacrifices they make to serve us, and I am grateful to be able to thank them in my own way

2. Spread smiles and happiness

Making someone smile is a simple yet powerful act that has the ability to brighten up someone's day and spread happiness. When you make someone smile, it not only impacts the recipient positively, but it can also boost your own mood and reduce stress.

Here are some ways to make someone smile:

Give Compliments: Complimenting someone on their appearance, work, or a specific trait can go a long way in making them feel good about themselves. How much effort does it take to complement someone?

'Dear reader, You are beautiful, kind and make a difference by reading this book. Your actions inspire change and bring hope to the world. Thank you for being a shining light.'

Doesn't it feel good?

Then why don't you do the same. From today compliment everyone with a good feeling in your heart. Give genuine compliment. I don't want you to lie dear reader. But give honest compliment. Every person has one or other good quality, appreciate them for it. I don't want you to lie to someone that they are beautiful, if you feel they are not then don't tell them they are beautiful. Everyone has a different perspective and interest. I may find someone beautiful who doesn't seem beautiful to you. There is no definition for beauty, It's different for everyone. You may like something or the other in a person. A person may be a good cook, a person may be a good singer, a person may have sweet voice. You must learn to compliment them for their good.

Are you ready to start doing it? I know you will forget because there is a lot I told. That's the reason I made a Check-sheet or a practice sheet which will help you to make a gradual change.

Share a joke or meme: Humor is a great way to lighten the mood and bring a smile to someone's face. Everyone may not be good at humor. Especially me. I am very poor with jokes. I always end up annoying people whenever I try to joke, But dear reader, the Intent matters. If you do something for a good intent. If you really take a step to make someone happy, they can feel it. Even if your joke doesn't work it's ok. Just be good and do good without thinking of the result. I'm doing same and working on my jokes. One day surely someone will laugh at my joke. One day surely, I'll have good Humor.

Ask about their day: Showing genuine interest in someone's life and asking how their day is going can make them feel appreciated and valued.

Offer to help: Offering to help someone with a task or problem can make them feel supported and less stressed.

Give a warm hug: Physical touch can have a positive impact on our emotional well-being, and a hug can be a comforting gesture that can bring a smile to someone's face.

Do a random act of kindness: Doing something kind for someone without expecting anything in return can brighten up their day and bring a smile to their face.

Making someone smile is a small act that can have a big impact. So, take a moment each day to bring a smile to someone's face and spread joy and positivity.

"If you think they are others,

You'll miss the feeling of brothers"

Social spark-plugs

Mini moves to ignite change

1. Orphanage and old age homes

Old people and Kids have a lot to teach and both of them have always been close to my heart. Kids teach us to innocently enjoy every aspect small or big about life and old people teach us what mistakes one must not do. They impart their experience to us and prevent us from doing mistakes they did.

I will share with you a story first and then tell you how you can do small things to enjoy your own life and also bring change in others life. Get ready for the story.

A Birthday with a Purpose:

The Journey to Celebrating with the Less Fortunate

Every year, I used to celebrate my birthday with just a handful of close friends. But one year, I decided to change my tradition and celebrate my special day in a unique way. I wanted to spread love and joy to those who needed it the most - the kids at an orphanage and the elderly at an ashram.

As I embarked on my mission, I faced several challenges. I had never visited an orphanage before, and I had no idea where to find one. I searched for nearby orphanages on Google Maps but all of them seemed too far away. I was unsure if they would even allow us to visit, let alone celebrate my birthday with the kids. But I didn't let those fears stop me. I called several orphanages and finally found one that welcomed us with open arms.

The next challenge was the logistics. How would we carry the cake, jalebis, mixture, chocolates, and juice all the way to the orphanage? But then I remembered that buying in bulk often leads to discounts, and so we ordered the cake from a nearby bakery, got chocolates and juice from Reliance Fresh, and bought a packet of mixture from a wholesale shop.

The day of the celebration arrived, and it was more beautiful than I could have ever imagined. The kids were overjoyed to see us and even more thrilled to receive treats and presents. I performed magic shows for them, and we spent hours chatting and laughing together. I was filled with an immense sense of happiness and fulfillment, knowing that I had made a difference in their lives, even if it was just for a day.

From that day on, I continued this tradition every year, on everyone's birthday. I wanted to spread the message that giving to others doesn't have to be expensive. It's the thought that counts, and the joy that we bring to others that truly makes it all worth it.

This will always be one of the most memorable and meaningful experiences of my life. It taught me the power of kindness and the true meaning of celebration - to spread love, joy, and hope to those who need it most. So, are you ready to incorporate this habit and start doing the same from today?

Let me tell you reasons why you should do it.

Bringing joy to those in need: Children living in orphanages and elderly people residing in old age homes may not have families or loved ones to celebrate their birthdays with. Celebrating birthdays in these facilities can bring a sense of joy, love, and belonging to these individuals who may otherwise feel neglected or forgotten. Your presence and celebration can make their day special and bring a smile to their faces.

Building community: Celebrating birthdays with others, regardless of age, can bring people together and foster a sense of community and belonging. This can be especially important for children living in orphanages and elderly people living in old age homes, who may not have many opportunities for social interaction. By celebrating birthdays with these individuals, you can help build relationships and a sense of community, which can have a positive impact on their well-being.

Providing a meaningful experience: Celebrating birthdays in orphanages and old age homes can be a fulfilling and meaningful experience for both the individuals being celebrated and for those doing the celebrating. It can provide a sense of purpose and a way to make a positive impact on the world, and can also be a way to connect with others and build relationships.

Raising awareness: Celebrating birthdays in these facilities can also raise awareness about the needs of orphans and elderly people, and encourage others to get involved in supporting these communities. By shining a light on the challenges faced by these individuals, you can help raise awareness and encourage others to get involved in supporting these communities.

Making a positive impact: By celebrating birthdays in orphanages and old age homes, you can have a positive impact on the lives of those you are celebrating with. This can include providing a sense of joy, love, and belonging, building community, and providing a meaningful experience. Additionally, by supporting these communities, you can contribute to creating a more inclusive and supportive society for all individuals, regardless of age or circumstance.

2. Hospitals

Have you felt the pain of being in a hospital. Do you know what patients feel. It's OK this story of mine will explain it to you.

The Magic of Smiles:

Bringing Hope to Hospital Patients

The hospital was a place of heartache and suffering. As I lay on my bed recovering from my surgery, I couldn't help but be struck by the countless other patients who were suffering far greater pains than my own. There was a young girl whose head had swelled to twice its normal size due to fluid buildup, and the sight of her agony broke my heart. Fear and worry hung thick in the air, casting a shadow over every bed in the ward. Everyone was desperate for some measure of hope and reassurance that they would make it through their ordeals, but those promises were few and far between.

But then I remembered something - that laughter is the best medicine. And so, I decided to use my skills as a magician to bring a little bit of joy into the hospital. I went from bed to bed, performing tricks and making the patients smile. It was a small act, but the impact it had was immense. I saw the fear in their eyes start to fade and the tightness in their chests loosen. They forgot, if only for a moment, the weight of their worries and allowed themselves to be fully present in the moment. It was a lesson that I would never forget.

Once my mother too was admitted to the hospital due to COVID, I saw first-hand the toll that the pandemic was taking on patients and their families. The fear was extreme, and it seemed like every day brought more news of loss and death. And everyone was in a state of fear. Beside my mom was an old lady who was very serious and could hardly breathe. Yet I found out no one taking care of her. But I knew that I had a duty to help in any way that I could. I sat by my mother's bedside and chatted with the elderly woman next to her, showing her a trick or two when she seemed down. And when I left that day, I felt like I had made a difference, even if only in a small way.

We all have skills and talents that we can use to help others. Whether it's magic tricks, storytelling, or just a listening ear, we can use our gifts to bring light into the lives of those who are struggling. The next time you find yourself in a hospital or a place of suffering, don't be afraid to use your unique abilities to make a difference. You never know how far-reaching the impact of your kindness might be.

So, what all can we do?

Visiting patients: Spending time with patients, either alone or in groups, can provide emotional support and help lift their spirits. Simply talking to them, playing games, or reading to them can be a great way to pass the time and bring a smile to their face. When visiting, it's important to be respectful of the patient's space and to follow any rules or guidelines set by the hospital staff.

Donating books, games, or crafts: Donating books, games, or crafting supplies can provide patients with a welcome distraction from their illness and help them pass the time. Consider donating items that are age-appropriate and suitable for the patient's interests. Books can be a great way to provide comfort and entertainment, and games or crafts can help keep the patient's mind occupied and active.

Bringing treats or meals: Patients in hospitals may not have access to good food or treats, so bringing them something special can be a great way to brighten their day. Consider bringing healthy snacks, fruits, or a homemade meal, and check with the hospital staff or the patient's family for any dietary restrictions.

Providing entertainment: If you have musical or artistic skills, you could bring a smile to a patient's face by playing music or drawing pictures for them. Consider offering to sing, play an instrument, or read a book to the patient. If you are an artist, you could offer to draw a picture or create a craft project with the patient.

Offering support: Patients in hospitals may be feeling overwhelmed, so offering a listening ear or a shoulder to cry on can be a great way to provide support and help lift their spirits. Be a comforting presence for the patient, and offer words of encouragement or hope. Sometimes just having someone to talk to can make a big difference.

Volunteering: Hospitals often have volunteer programs that allow people to assist with tasks such as running errands, playing with children, or just providing a friendly face. Participating in these programs can be a great way to bring a smile to a patient's face and support the hospital staff. Consider volunteering your time and skills to make a difference in the lives of patients and their families.

"A single step, taken with heart and might,

Can lead to change that shines as bright as light."

National navigators

Mini milestones to move your country forward

1. Cleanliness

All of us complain about the condition of our country. We complain about the situation. But that the major problem with people, we complain but don't take any action. Let's dive back into a story and understand how I took a small step and changed myself.

Magician and the dustbin:

A journey of mindset change

Once upon a time in my college during my PUC, Here in Bangalore we call 11th and 12th class as Pre-university, so during my pre - university college I used to show people magic tricks. I had learned to perform magic and whenever I was late to college and was not allowed to enter the class, I used to show people magic outside. My college life was beautiful. Got a lot of respect from everyone. But one day I was eating biscuit and drinking juice. After I finished eating the biscuit, I threw the packet down. I always used to do that and never looked for dustbin. But that day a girl sitting there saw me. She called out "Hello, Hello". I responded "Yes". She asked what is this. I asked "What". she told "what did you just do?"

I didn't realize what she was talking about. Then she scolded me and told me to pick the cover and throw it into the dustbin. I felt insulted at first and was angry at her. But then I realized it is my college and I must keep it clean. And then on I started to keep place clean and not dump garbage everywhere. I realized it doesn't take much effort to go walk up to the dustbin and throw the thrash. This small incident changed my mindset. It might not have been a big thing. That girl wouldn't even have realized what a big change she has brought. She just told it casually but that changed a person. And today I tell others and this makes it a chain. If you start telling people and if you do such a small act of throwing thrash in dustbin it can change a lot of people and it can thereby even change the country.

Here are some ways you can contribute to keeping your country clean:

Reduce waste: Minimize the amount of waste you produce by recycling, composting, and reducing the use of single-use plastics. Be mindful of the packaging you choose and try to purchase products that come in recyclable or biodegradable packaging.

Litter control: Participate in community litter cleanups and dispose of litter properly, either by placing it in a trash can or recycling bin. Encourage others to do the same, and educate them about the impact of litter on the environment.

Water conservation: Conserve water by fixing leaks, taking shorter showers, and using drought-resistant plants in your landscaping. Reduce the amount of water you use in your daily life, and be mindful of water waste.

Energy conservation: Reduce your energy consumption by using energy-efficient appliances, turning off lights when you leave a room, and setting your thermostat to an energy-saving temperature. Consider using renewable energy sources, such as solar power, to reduce your carbon footprint.

Proper disposal of hazardous waste: Properly dispose of hazardous waste, such as chemicals, batteries, and electronic waste, to prevent contamination of soil and water. Check with your local waste management authority for information on how to dispose of these items properly.

Encourage others: Encourage your friends, family, and community members to join you in keeping your country clean. Lead by example and educate others about the importance of environmental responsibility.

So, From now on start keeping your surrounding clean. If you don't find a dustbin don't complain and blame the state for it. Don't dump garbage anywhere, Just carry it with you in your pocket or in your bag and throw it in your house in your dustbin. It takes a small change to change the system and the nation. Start from it today

2. Helping the poor

What do you think when it comes about helping beggars. Let's see what I used to think about them.

The Beggar's Lesson:

A Journey of Empathy

I was a heartless person, always scowling at beggars and feeling indignant towards them. "Why can't they just work hard and earn their own living?" I used to grumble.

One day, a visit to a beautiful temple in Talakadu, As I walked out of one of the many temples, an old beggar woman approached me, pleading for money. My anger boiled over, and I was ready to lash out. My friends noticed my fury and quickly intervened, one of them grabbing my hand and gently imploring me to calm down.

"Rajat, don't be angry. Shouting or scolding her won't change anything," my friend reasoned.

But I was obstinate, fuming at the audacity of this beggar to follow me and ask for money. "Why should I give her anything? I work hard for every penny I earn, why can't she do the same?" I retorted.

I thought of the countless elderly people selling goods and the handicapped workers in industries, striving to make ends meet despite their hardships. "These beggars are fit and able, why do they beg instead of working?" I ranted.

But my friend's words finally penetrated my stubborn heart. "We can't do anything about it, Rajat. Ignoring her is the best option."

I know that you might be thinking what a cruel person I am. May be that lady really had problems, maybe she really couldn't work. She was old anyways; I should have at least not got angry and respected her at least for her age. YES, you are right "dear reader" I feel the same too when I think of myself and how I used to reacted. But let me tell you the reason why I started to hate beggars.

One day after my classes when I stepped outside my college. I was hungry as usual and bought butter fruit milkshake near my college. I was drank the juice and ate a packet of biscuit and was returning home. Then I saw a person. He was drunk. He had torn clothes. He was walking on the opposite side of the road to which I was walking. But then suddenly I saw something which surprised me. I never thought someone could do that. That person opened his shirt button. I was wondering what he's going to do and then he put one of his hand inside his shirt and closed the button. I was wondering why he did so. Then I saw few girls walking front of him. This person then started begging them for money. People thought he has no arm and gave him money. This Incident made me angry. I started to think every beggar begs for money and then goes to bar and drinks.

But wait this is not the end. This was just a beginning. Next, I walked toward bus stop to return home. I saw few of my friends and started walking with them. Then a transgender approached us and asked for money. I was a person who didn't give money so I ignored her, But my friend who had a kind heart took out his wallet to give her the money and as he held his wallet to give her money. Guess what happened!

She snatched his wallet and started to run. Luckily, we saw a police standing near Bus-stop we told him and he ran towards her and slapped her. He took the wallet from her and gave it back. So, this made me hate beggars more.

But is this the end? Shouldn't we help poor? Am I still cruel?

No that is not the end. For almost a year I hated beggars and disrespected them. Until one day, when I saw a video on YouTube. He was a person who said a beautiful line which changed my entire mindset. He quoted-

"Always do monetary charity. And do it without any intention in mind. Never think what the person will do with the money. Don't try to justify not helping someone by telling that he will drink. Help people for who you are. Help people because you are good. Don't judge people. Don't try to be their dad. If someone drinks with your money it's his problem. He's spoiling his life, If he uses it good way it's his choice. Just because of our judgement we might end up not helping the people who actually deserve. so Help everyone with whatever you can. If people use it wrong way they will suffer, at least there will be a happiness inside you that you did something with good intent."

These lines touched me. I realized that I'm no one to judge everyone just because of two incidents that I saw. Everyone may not be like that. And this made me love everyone. I Stopped Judging people and helped everyone who asked me for help. This helped me becoming a better person and today I want to help the Reader of this book.

What are the ways in which you can help the poor?

Volunteering: Volunteering is a great way to directly help people in need and support organizations that serve them. When you volunteer, you can donate your time, skills, and energy to a cause you care about. For example, you could volunteer at a local soup kitchen, help with meal distribution at a homeless shelter, or assist with after-school programs for children from low-income families. Volunteering is a great way to make a difference in your community and build relationships with others who share your values.

Donating money: Financial donations can make a significant impact in the lives of people living in poverty. You can donate directly to a charity or non-profit organization that helps people in need, or you can choose to give to a specific cause, such as providing food, housing, or healthcare. When you donate money, you can also claim a tax deduction, depending on your country's tax laws.

Donating goods: Donating goods, such as clothing, household items, and food, can also help people in need. Many organizations, such as shelters and food banks, rely on donations to help those in need. Consider hosting a drive in your community to collect these items and make a difference in the lives of people living in poverty.

Advocating: Advocating for policies and programs that support people living in poverty is another way to help. This can involve speaking out about the issue, writing letters to elected officials, and participating in community events and campaigns. By advocating for change, you can help raise awareness about poverty and work to create a more just and equitable society.

Mentoring or tutoring: Offering your time and skills to mentor or tutor someone who is struggling can make a big difference in their life. You can help with job search skills, financial planning, or school work. By offering your support, you can help someone gain the skills and knowledge they need to improve their circumstances and achieve their goals.

Educating yourself: Learning about the root causes of poverty and the ways in which it affects people and communities is an important step in helping to reduce poverty. By educating yourself, you can gain a deeper understanding of the issue and be better equipped to advocate for change. Share what you learn with others and work to raise awareness about poverty and its impact.

Supporting small businesses: Supporting small businesses owned by people living in poverty is another way to help. By purchasing their products and services, you can help these entrepreneurs create jobs, build their businesses, and improve their financial security.

Organizing a fundraiser: Organizing a fundraiser, such as a walk or a bake sale, can help raise money for organizations that help people in need. By bringing people together to support a common cause, you can make a significant impact in the lives of those in need. Fundraisers can also be a great way to raise awareness about poverty and its impact

So did you realize that you shouldn't lose your values and your character by judging people. Because of my mindset I thought of insulting an old women. I insulted elders who were elder than me only because they were begging. I realized finally that I was against my ethics. My thinking made me do wrong. I respect every beggar nowadays and help them. Because a small donation doesn't make me lose anything.

"To see a nation, reach its shining crest,

Its people must come together and do their best."

Global game changers

Micro actions for a macro impact

1. Be a Vegan

Now I want you to imagine something. Imagine

Born into a cruel world, you enter the world in a small, suffocating room. The day you are born, you are cruelly locked away in a cramped cage, surrounded by countless others who share your fate. The air is thick, and you struggle to breathe as you take in your surroundings. Your legs are wobbly, and you can barely stand, yet you are forced to endure the harsh conditions.

The screams of your mother pierce through the air, and you watch in horror as she is brutally murdered right before your eyes. Her blood spills onto the floor, her head is hacked off, and her body convulses as the life is drained from her. You are powerless to stop it, a mere witness to the cruelty of humanity.

And just when you thought it couldn't get any worse, the next day you lay your eyes on your sister. You may be too young to comprehend what is happening, but you can feel the fear and terror in the air. The screams of your sister join the chorus of those who have suffered before you.

You are trapped, a prisoner in your own body, forced to endure the atrocities around you. This is because you are baby chicken, baby goat or A baby calf and not as cute as a dog or a cat who are treated like kings or queens just because they are cute. This is called speciesism, the process of treating one species differently than others. There is no difference between this and racism.

Do you know this was the situation of slaves once upon a time. It was the situation of black people. But they could fight. They were as powerful as us. This was the situation of lower caste people.

But why didn't normal people fight? Why didn't people realize something is wrong and stop exploiting them.

Because it was a part of the system. Once you see something from the childhood and you are born with it, You realize that is normal. You think being mistreated and being used is your fate. And the people who did it think it is their right. People use terms like God created lower class people for us, etc. Just like what you do with some animals today and you feel it's right for you to do it to please your tongue because you have done it from birth.

But you know whom we remember and thank today? We remember Nelson Mandela and Dr.B.R Ambedkar. Because they were different. They could realize what is wrong.

I know all of you must be thinking that you would have done the same thing or at least you would not have mistreated the lower caste people like everyone did. You think you would have understood what is wrong and would have helped them.

But "dear reader" aren't you doing the same thing? Aren't you torturing the ones weaker than you. Aren't you exploiting them today? Aren't you thinking you are superior and not caring about their family and torturing them.?

Non veg... We think we are superior animals and can put animals in cage. We can exploit the animals. Rip their skin and enjoy their flesh without hearing their screams. We feel it's right because everyone does it. But Can we not bring the change?

Should we argue with people telling Vague statements like Plants feel pain too...

Animals have a nervous system and nervous system makes us feel pain. We studied in our younger class about sense organs. Plants don't have sense organs and animals are like us who has sense organs and skin to feel pain. Why are we breeding animals for us?

Eating flesh fills us with bad emotions. Because when the animal dies its is filled with fear, pain, anger and other negative emotions. When you consume it these negativities enter you. So to improve your personal life stop consuming negativity. Stop harming animals only to please your tongue. Pulses, Dals and other vegetables have all required amino acids and proteins. Stop giving that as a reason.

"Lets start being a human and start showing humanity."

I can write an entire book why it is wrong to be a non-vegetarian, But since this book is about changing world I will talk only things related to that.

I already told you how being a vegan and stopping animal products can help you at personal level. But how can it change world.

A. Climate change

Veganism can play a role in reducing the impacts of climate change by reducing greenhouse gas (GHG) emissions and land use changes associated with animal agriculture. Some of the ways in which this can occur are:

Livestock Agriculture: Livestock farming is a significant contributor to GHG emissions, particularly methane and nitrous oxide, which are potent greenhouse gases. Cows and sheep are the primary producers of methane through digestion and manure decomposition, while nitrous oxide is produced by fertilized soil and manure management. Reducing the demand for animal products can help to reduce these emissions.

Deforestation: Land is often cleared for grazing and to grow crops to feed livestock, contributing to deforestation and habitat loss. By reducing the demand for animal products, veganism can help to reduce the need for this type of land use change

Water Usage: Animal agriculture is a significant user of water resources. It takes large amounts of water to grow crops to feed livestock and to provide water for the animals themselves. By reducing the demand for animal products, veganism can help to reduce water usage.

Land Use Changes: Livestock farming can lead to the conversion of forests, grasslands, and other ecosystems into agricultural land. By reducing the demand for animal products, veganism can help to reduce the need for these types of land use changes.

B. World health

All of you know how the pandemic started. COVID had a major impact on our life. Whole world suffered and it all started with bats. If people didn't consume bats the world wouldn't have suffered. Other ways how vegan diet can help solve world health is

Heart Health: A plant-based diet rich in fruits, vegetables, whole grains, and legumes has been associated with a reduced risk of heart disease. This is likely due to the fact that vegan diets are often low in saturated fat and high in fiber, antioxidants, and phytochemicals, which have a protective effect on heart health.

Chronic Disease Prevention: A vegan diet has been linked to a reduced risk of several chronic diseases, including type 2 diabetes, certain cancers, and high blood pressure. This may be due to the fact that plant-based diets are typically high in fiber, vitamins, minerals, and antioxidants, and low in unhealthy fats and processed foods.

Weight Management: A well-planned vegan diet can be an effective way to manage weight and maintain a healthy body weight. Plant-based diets are often lower in calories and higher in fiber, which can help with weight control.

Improved Gut Health: A vegan diet can also improve gut health by increasing the diversity of gut bacteria, which can have positive effects on overall health.

It's important to note that while a vegan diet can be healthy and nutritionally adequate.

C. World Hunger

The production of animal-based foods is a significant drain on global food resources and can contribute to world hunger in several ways. Some of these ways include:

Resource Allocation: A large portion of the world's crops and resources are used to produce food for animals, rather than for direct human consumption. For example, it takes several pounds of grain to produce just one pound of meat, meaning that a lot of food resources are being diverted from human consumption to feed animals. If these resources were redirected to grow crops for direct human consumption, it could help to reduce world hunger.

Land Use Changes: Land is often cleared for grazing and to grow crops to feed livestock, contributing to deforestation and habitat loss. This can displace local communities and reduce the availability of fertile land for food production, potentially exacerbating world hunger.

Water Usage: Animal agriculture is a significant user of water resources. It takes large amounts of water to grow crops to feed livestock and to provide water for the animals themselves. This can strain water resources and reduce the availability of water for other uses, including agriculture for human consumption.

By reducing the demand for animal-based foods, veganism can help to redirect resources towards direct human consumption and potentially reduce world hunger. It's important to note that while veganism can play a role in reducing world hunger, it is not a silver bullet solution. A comprehensive approach is needed, including increased food production and distribution, and addressing issues such as poverty and unequal distribution of resources.

This is how veganism can solve world problems. So, take your step towards change.

"With each meal that's free from animal pain,

We take a step towards a world that's more sustain."

Conclusion

I told a lot of things one has to do to change the world. But the biggest role in a person's life is Played by his parents, teachers and friends. I never made a lot of friends because I always believed in Quality and not quantity. All the friends I have are from the school time. I never made friends in later stages of my life. Even if I did, they were temporary and I didn't stay in-touch with them.

Once upon a time we had been given a project. A science project in our school. We were a group of three friends who decided to do it together. For now, Let's call my friends Mr. G and Mr. A.Mr. G was my best friend from the beginning, may be because our birthday was on the same day. Ok Ok dear reader, I know joke isn't funny I told you I'm poor with jokes. But Yes Mr. G had Birthday on the same day. So, we were doing the project and we had to go here and there in search of materials. I was with my friend G and then A called me. He asked me Rajat, where are you. We picked up the call and told him that we are at our Science teachers home. We told him that our science sir is helping us do the project. And I cut the call-in hurry telling that my battery is low. Dear reader, Our science teacher was the most strict teacher anyone can have. He used to hit the students very hard and used to get angry easily. A normal human would not trust when I told him I am at my strictest teacher's home but this Mr. A was a genius and he thought we were really at teacher's home. He didn't realize I was just pranking him. He immediately went to the teachers home and started peeping through his window. And unfortunately, when he looked back, He saw the teacher standing behind him. Sir asked him Why are you peeping through my window. My friend A told him I was seeing Rajat and Mr.G through your window. That day Mr. A got a lot of scolding and next day sir complained to my principal and told her that He was peeping through my window and He says he did so because of Rajat and G. Then principal asked us Is it true Rajat? I told no, I was busy in doing project. You can see my project I have completed it. Do you think I would have had time for all these. Then principal punished him. It was not very serious. We did it for fun. So, I agree I did wrong But that's friendship and there is nothing right and wrong in it. Even today we recall that incident and laugh loudly. Still today all three of us are best friends. Some incidents create beautiful memories.

I think you might have realized how naughty I was in my childhood.

My pharmacy college along with best teachers also gave me a sister. I never had a sister and always wanted a sister. My lab partner in my college used to irritate me a lot. We used to fight a lot and got punished from the teacher many times. She is a girl who was a best person to be my sister. She always cared and fought with me like sisters do. So I always feel thankful to my college to have given me the best teacher like my Anatomy sir who always guided me and a sister.

My school gave me Friends for life, My 11th and 12th class gave me a ghostie for life, My Pharmacy college gave me a sister for life.

And collectively I also got best teachers.

Why am I telling all of these?

I am telling all of these to explain you the value of people around you. The people around you are responsible for who you become. I had a friend who used to travel by cycle and sometime walk just to meet me. I always feel lucky when I think of these people. I keep these people carefully and close to my heart.

My friends, My teachers, My parents, My sister and my brother all did a lot for me. I can never give them as much as they did for me.

One day I will die trying to be perfect student, brother, friend and a perfect son. But I'm sure My book will always be alive in the homes of people and will always guide people in becoming the best version of themself and creating a better world.

I have Put a check sheet which gives you in steps how you can change your life. It is a complete 30-day routine to make everything I said a habit in your life. It will help you to incorporate all the teachings in your life.

Dear reader, I hope I have been a good teacher and a guide to you. Welcome to my family. Thank you for choosing to change the world and taking a step to create a better world.

Check-sheets

Monthly Check-sheet

Every night put a tick near the day if you completed all the tasks that were told to you to do that day. If you miss a day start from the next table all from the beginning considering it as first day.

Day 1	Day 2	Day 3	Day 4	Day 5	Day 6	Day 7
Day 8	Day 9	Day 10	Day 11	Day 12	Day 13	Day 14
Day 15	Day 16	Day 17	Day 18	Day 19	Day 20	Day 21
Day 22	Day 23	Day 24	Day 25	Day 26	Day 27	Day 28
Day 29	Day 30	Day 31	**If you skip a day start all over from beginning**			

Day 1	Day 2	Day 3	Day 4	Day 5	Day 6	Day 7
Day 8	Day 9	Day 10	Day 11	Day 12	Day 13	Day 14
Day 15	Day 16	Day 17	Day 18	Day 19	Day 20	Day 21

Day 22	Day 23	Day 24	Day 25	Day 26	Day 27	Day 28
Day 29	Day 30	Day 31	**If you skip a day start all over from beginning**			

Day 1	Day 2	Day 3	Day 4	Day 5	Day 6	Day 7
Day 8	Day 9	Day 10	Day 11	Day 12	Day 13	Day 14
Day 15	Day 16	Day 17	Day 18	Day 19	Day 20	Day 21
Day 22	Day 23	Day 24	Day 25	Day 26	Day 27	Day 28
Day 29	Day 30	Day 31	**If you skip a day start all over from beginning**			

Day 1	Day 2	Day 3	Day 4	Day 5	Day 6	Day 7
Day 8	Day 9	Day 10	Day 11	Day 12	Day 13	Day 14
Day 15	Day 16	Day 17	Day 18	Day 19	Day 20	Day 21
Day 22	Day 23	Day 24	Day 25	Day 26	Day 27	Day 28
Day 29	Day 30	Day 31	**If you skip a day start all over from beginning**			

Small Changes, Great Impact

Day 1	Day 2	Day 3	Day 4	Day 5	Day 6	Day 7
Day 8	Day 9	Day 10	Day 11	Day 12	Day 13	Day 14
Day 15	Day 16	Day 17	Day 18	Day 19	Day 20	Day 21
Day 22	Day 23	Day 24	Day 25	Day 26	Day 27	Day 28
Day 29	Day 30	Day 31	**If you skip a day start all over from beginning**			

Day 1	Day 2	Day 3	Day 4	Day 5	Day 6	Day 7
Day 8	Day 9	Day 10	Day 11	Day 12	Day 13	Day 14
Day 15	Day 16	Day 17	Day 18	Day 19	Day 20	Day 21
Day 22	Day 23	Day 24	Day 25	Day 26	Day 27	Day 28
Day 29	Day 30	Day 31	**If you skip a day start all over from beginning**			

Day 1	Day 2	Day 3	Day 4	Day 5	Day 6	Day 7
Day 8	Day 9	Day 10	Day 11	Day 12	Day 13	Day 14
Day 15	Day 16	Day 17	Day 18	Day 19	Day 20	Day 21
Day 22	Day 23	Day 24	Day 25	Day 26	Day 27	Day 28
Day 29	Day 30	Day 31	**If you skip a day start all over from beginning**			

Be serious because successful people are hustlers and they always follow the plan. If you fail at basic things then you cannot achieve bigger thing. Hope you will achieve success in your journey. I have Put the daily goals in the next page. Follow them and Tick on the check-sheet only if you are successful

Daily Targets and Sheets:

Note: Incorporating a new habit can be challenging, but one effective strategy is to associate it with something else you already do regularly. This helps to create a cue for the new habit, making it easier to remember and integrate into your daily routine. For example, if you want to start meditating in the morning, you could associate it with brushing your teeth. Every time you brush your teeth, you would also do your meditation. Over time, the habit of meditating in the morning becomes automatic, and you no longer need to rely on the cue of brushing your teeth to remember to do it. By linking the new habit to a pre-existing routine, you can increase the chances of making it a consistent part of your daily life. And also remember not to continue other things later unless you followed the daily target. Give yourself punishment. Initially when I started these things I made sure I would meditate immediately after waking up and brushing my teeth. Brushing teeth was a reminder to meditate and I decided I will not have my breakfast until I did meditation no matter how late how I got to college. You must decide strongly that you will postpone the breakfast or skip your work If you missed the routine and decide that you will only continue normal life after you are done. So Here are the targets:

DAY 1

Meditation-

Decide a time of the day when you want to do meditation, I suggest you early mornings are best when the world is quiet. But you can do it at any time of the day.

1. Time at which I will meditate daily?

   _____a.m or p.m

2. How was your experience after meditating today? How did you feel? Write down In detail what happened during the process and if you could focus.

3. How long could you do it?

　　　　　　　　 minutes

Day 2

Meditation

Today's goal- Trying to do it longer than yesterday

1. Could you do longer than yesterday with less distraction??

Yes/ No

2. How was your experience after meditating today? How did you feel? Write down In detail what happened during the process and if you could focus.

_____
_____
_____
_____

3. How long could you do it?

   _____ minutes

Day 3

Meditation

Today's goal- Doing longer than yesterday and focusing on breathe and at the Centre of the head. Can also use a positive phrase or a mantra and repeat it in your head.

1. Could you do longer than yesterday with less distraction??

Yes/ No

2. How was your experience after meditating today? How did you feel? Write down In detail what happened during the process and if you could focus.

_____
_____
_____
_____
_____
_____
_____
_____
_____
_____

3. How long could you do it?

   _____minutes

Day 4

Meditation and breathing exercise.

Today's goal- Do breathing exercise before your meditation. That will also prepare you for meditation and help improve meditation.

1. How did you feel doing Breathing exercise?

   _____
   _____
   _____
   _____

2. Which breathing exercise did you do?

   _____
   _____

3. Could you do longer than yesterday with less distraction??

Yes/ No

1. How was your experience after meditating today? How did you feel? Write down In detail what happened during the process and if you could focus.

   _____
   _____
   _____
   _____
   _____

_____
_____
_____
_____

_____

2. How long could you do it?

_____minutes

Day 5

Breathing exercise and Meditation

Today's goal- To do better than yesterday

How was your day yesterday? Did meditation and Breathing exercise make you feel a change?

Yes/No,

_____
_____

_____

Day 6

It's time to incorporate Bhagavad gita in your life. You can do it Before sleep. Or after Meditation

1. How is Breathing exercise and meditation going? Also Write how much improvement you made at it

_____
_____
_____

2. When did you read Bhagavad gita?

3. How much did you read? And what did you learn?

Day 7

1. How is Breathing exercise and meditation going? Also Write how much improvement you made at it

2. How much did you read? And what did you learn?

_____

_____

_____

DAY 8

Start doing any basic exercise or join a gym.

Can do it in the evenings, but I feel better when I do it after my meditation. I take rest and go to gym and it makes me do better and push my limits.

Did You realize you are weak. Did you realize the value of the book?

Did you get exhausted soon in the gym?

That is an Indication that your body has become weak due to lack of exercise.

Note- Try to Start consuming healthy, yet vegetarian food, since non veg is harmful to world and also to your body. It makes your body acidic which invites lot of diseases.

1. Did you go to gym or workout at home?

_____

2. How do you feel exercising today?

_____

_____

3. How was your meditation and breathing exercise?

_____

4. How is Breathing exercise and meditation going? Also Write how much improvement you made at it

_____
_____
_____
_____
_____

5. How much did you read? And what did you learn?

_____
_____
_____
_____
_____
_____
_____
___

Day 9

1. How do you feel exercising today?

_____
_____

2. How was your meditation and breathing exercise?

_____

3. How is Breathing exercise and meditation going? Also Write how much improvement you made at it

_____
_____
_____

4. How much did you read? And what did you learn?

Day 10

1. How do you feel exercising today?

2. How was your meditation and breathing exercise?

3. How is Breathing exercise and meditation going? Also Write how much improvement you made at it

4. How much did you read? And what did you learn?

Day 11

Time to change the community now. Let's start gratitude.

Today's goal - Thank all the shopkeepers from you purchase things. Immediate after they handover the thing to you tell thank you with a smile. Also try to tell your teacher, your manager, your parents, your kid or anyone around you for anything they do.

1. Mention the people you thanked today, How they reacted and how you felt after it.

2. How was your Breathing exercise, Meditation and exercise? How much did you improve.

Small Changes, Great Impact

Day 12

Try to thank more number of people than you did yesterday.

4. Mention the people you thanked today, How they reacted and how you felt after it.

_____
_____
_____
_____
_____
_____
_____
_____
_____

5. How was your Breathing exercise, Meditation and exercise? How much did you improve.

_____
_____
_____
_____

Day 13

1. Mention the people you thanked today, How they reacted and how you felt after it.

_____
_____
_____

2. How was your Breathing exercise, Meditation and exercise? How much did you improve

Day 14

1. Mention the people you thanked today, How they reacted and how you felt after it.

2. How was your Breathing exercise, Meditation and exercise? How much did you improve

Day 15

1. Mention the people you thanked today, How they reacted and how you felt after it.

2. How was your Breathing exercise, Meditation and exercise? How much did you improve

Day 16

Make at least one person smile. You can go prepared from the Internet for joke.

1. Who was the person that you cracked the joke. Did they smile? What was the joke?

   _____
   _____
   _____
   _____
   _____

2. Mention the people you thanked today, How they reacted and how you felt after it.

   _____
   _____
   _____
   _____
   _____
   _____
   _____
   _____
   _____

3. How was your Breathing exercise, Meditation and exercise? How much did you improve

   _____
   _____
   _____
   _____

Day 17

Make more than one person smile. Try to include a stranger or the shopkeeper you thanked.

1. Who was the person that you cracked the joke. Did they smile? What was the joke?

   _____
   _____
   _____
   _____
   _____

2. Mention the people you thanked today, How they reacted and how you felt after it.

   _____
   _____
   _____
   _____
   _____
   _____
   _____
   _____
   _____

3. How was your Breathing exercise, Meditation and exercise? How much did you improve

   _____
   _____
   _____

Day 18

Make more than one person smile.

1. Who were the people that you spread smile to??

   _____

   _____

   _____

   _____

   _____

2. Have you started feeling a change in you?

   Yes/ no

3. What is the change?

   _____

   _____

   _____

   _____

4. Mention the people you thanked today, How they reacted and how you felt after it.

   _____

   _____

   _____

5. How was your Breathing exercise, Meditation and exercise? How much did you improve

   _____

   _____

   _____

   _____

Day 19 and 20 continue the same.

Day 21

Visit an Old age home and celebrate even if it is not an occasion. Share chocolates or anything good with them. Celebrate because you have improved and become a different person. You can take your friends or family with you.

Warning - Please don't skip this step Since it's a most effective change and the most important step to personal and social welfare.

1. Write Down your experience

_____
_____
_____
_____
_____
_____
_____

_____

I know these many lines may not be enough to describe the feeling. You can write it down in a book and take an oath

"I will always celebrate all important occasions in old age homes or orphanages"

Day 22

same as day 18

1. Who were the people that you spread smile to??

_____
_____
_____
_____
_____

2. Have you started feeling a change in you?

Yes/ no

3. What is the change?

_____
_____
_____
_____

4. Mention the people you thanked today, How they reacted and how you felt after it.

_____
_____
_____
_____
_____
_____
_____
_____
_____

5. How was your Breathing exercise, Meditation and exercise? How much did you improve

_____
_____
_____
_____

Day 23

same

1. Who were the people that you spread smile to??

_____
_____
_____
_____
_____

2. Have you started feeling a change in you?

Yes/ no

3. What is the change?

_____
_____
_____
_____

4. Mention the people you thanked today, How they reacted and how you felt after it.

_____
_____
_____

___

___

___

___

___

___

___

5. How was your Breathing exercise, Meditation and exercise? How much did you improve

___

___

___

___

Day 24

Don't throw garbage on the roads and carry it at home or throw it in a dustbin outside. If you already follow it tell one person who is doing it and stop him from littering. It could be a friend or a stranger.

1. Did you do it?

Yes/ No

Day 25

Give a beggar some money. Even if it is as little as 10 rs

1. Did you do it?

yes/no

Day 26

Stop another person from littering

1. Did you do it?

yes/ no

Day 27

Give a traffic police, police office, bus conductor or a social worker a packet of biscuit and a small bottle of juice and thank them for working in the sun and serving us

It takes lot of effort and courage to do it. And it completes two tasks. It helps the poor and also shows gratitude. So Don't miss to do it.

1. Did you do it?

2. Did you feel afraid to approach them?

3. How do you feel after achieving it?

4. How did they react?

Day 28

Start keeping a diary and writing down these things before you sleep

Day 29

Share this book with your friend or gift them a new one. If you don't want to do it at least share your leanings with them and try to bring a change in them too.

and finally, Day 30

Visit a hospital and ask for permission from the staff to let you interact with the patients. Talk to them and spend some time with them. Be prepared to go with some jokes to tell them.

1. How did you feel?

This will teach you the value of life and how we take our health for granted. It will motivate you to focus on health and respect the beautiful body you have and will also encourage you to stick with whatever I told in the book.

You have changed and become a better person. Not everyone can achieve these. You are a good person.

Thank you for buying this book and being a part of my family.

www.ingramcontent.com/pod-product-compliance
Lightning Source LLC
LaVergne TN
LVHW041613070526
838199LV00052B/3130